This Thing Called

Life ...

Embrace It

Volume I: An Introduction to Life

Ki O'Shea

LifeRich
PUBLISHING

LifeRich Publishing is a registered trademark of
The Reader's Digest Association, Inc.

LifeRich Publishing books may be ordered through booksellers or by contacting:

LifeRich Publishing
1663 Liberty Drive
Bloomington, IN 47403
www.liferichpublishing.com
1 (888) 238-8637

Interior Image Credit: Anthony Shaun Davis

ISBN: 978-1-4897-2293-5 (sc)
ISBN: 978-1-4897-2291-1 (hc)
ISBN: 978-1-4897-2292-8 (e)

Library of Congress Control Number: 2019906750

Print information available on the last page.

LifeRich Publishing rev. date: 11/05/2019

FOREWORD

Often times relationships are formed. How and why they happen are sometimes unknown, you just know that they (it) happened. This is our story. Looking back, I can honestly say that I do not know how our relationship happened, I just know that it did, and I thank God for it. But of course, if you would ask her, she would say something totally different. She may just say, this thing called life. In true Ki-fashion, if she says that she's going to do something, she does. This thing called life has been Ki's baby for at least a decade now. At that time, I wasn't sure of the avenue that the expression would be used, but I was certain that it would be. When Ki finished law school from Charlotte's School of Law, she gifted members of her support system a shirt that read "this thing called life." Over the years, things happened. Some were expected, others were not. Some good, some not so much.

North Carolina Agricultural and Technical State University
Office of Undergraduate Admissions
1601 East Market Street, Greensboro, NC 27411

But through it all, she held strong, persevered and continue to live out her dreams. Anyone that knows that she has a gift of gab, loves people, enjoys reading and traveling and to receive hand written notes. Over the last year she has found away to combine many of her loves and now shares them with the world through her blogs. This Thing called Life is a compilation of many of her experiences and I am happy that She has allowed me to tag a long.

Love you, Mean It.

Jikele W. Evans

North Carolina Agricultural and Technical State University
Office of Undergraduate Admissions
1601 East Market Street, Greensboro, NC 27411

To my "Oprah." "This Thing Called Life" is an ongoing drive that has many straight aways, winds, turns and bends. During the straight aways we laugh, smile, love and have fun. The winds, turns and bends make us grieve, cry and lament. My closest friend and I know these moments too well. Our abusive past has given a rise to insight on how the world should truly be. We share a love for people and pour out our hearts with enduring gifts. Kwi(kiera) has a smile that can light up any room. Her warmth shines in the midst of racism, social injustice and a broken education system. As educators, we remain dedicated to our students, but struggle with the systems that holds them back. "Love" is the key to life. "This Thing Called Life" is not possible without love. Thank you for the love we have shared for over 20 years. The teacher and student continue to switch roles in order to maintain educational harmony. We came from the bottom to the "top! Oh "This Thing Called Life."

Hey mom,

First off I am extremley proud of you. You finished
one of your adventures in "This Thing Called Life",
and it's only going to get better from here.
Next I Love you! I Love you a lot! You instil so much
into me, ratter it be values, lessons, morals, inspiration,
or love you do it, and you do it well. You teach me
many things. You taught me to hold the door for me
person behind you, how to wash clothes and even
write a letter like this one. I appreciate you,
the whole world appreciates you and how you
do things. You're the definition of a leader and
you lead well. So now after we celebrate this step into
your life journey we will move on? What's next? Dentistry?
Haha, I'm just kidding, unless... But in all seriousness
I love you and I see this big accomplishment in your
career and think, it's only the beginning!! Kiera O'shea,
you are GREATNESS in the making!!

Love, Best son ANTHONY

Well Hello K...!!

To say that I am proud is an understatement. I definitely remember one first time we met and you are still as sweet now as you were back then to this displaced college freshman whose dream of going to NC A&T SU was slowly unfolding. God knew exactly what he was doing when he placed us in each other's path. I have truly enjoyed watching your accomplishments happen despite the numerous times life has knocked you down. "This Thing Called Life" has truly been an inspiration to me and I am beyond honored to let you and the world know how much I love you and look forward to what's next!! Congratulations!!

-Sister

My Lottery Winnings
My Gayle
My Oprah
My Glinda

I believe everything happens
for a reason and no matter the
magnitude of our challenges, we
are capable to achieve it.
Throughout all of my accomplishments
and down falls you have been
there for me. You have been
around my entire 20s decade
and right now you are still here!
A Lifetime to go! As you know
it was NOT easy but I made
everything possible because of
you with your uplifting and
positive spirit. I am so grateful
for you. I still remember the
day I asked you to be my mentor.
Since then, I was stuck to you
like glue! I don't know why but
it was the best decision I ever
made! Kiera, your love is so
contagious! "This thing called

life" is filled with everything
and more. It is never perfect.
You reminded me to take it for
what it is and embrace the
goodness of it. You reminded me
to love and be patient with
opening my heart to others,
(even when I didn't want to)
Who would have known that
not only did I gain a mentor,
I have my own Gayle/Oprah
in my "small but awesome" circle!
My very own Glinda telling me
to click my heels three times
to go "home". You are simply
amazing in everything that
you do and more. No one can
take that from you. So inspiring!
You are definitely like hitting
the jack pot and I am taking
all the winnings ♡

With love,

Jayla

INTRODUCTION

What is ThisThingCalledLife…
(Do I really need a
question mark?)

Dear Reader,

I realized some time ago that life is as complicated as we make it. Life hurts us. Life tests us. Life makes us cry. Life makes us laugh. Life also frustrates us. It also scares us; as a matter of fact, it might scare us so bad that we become anxious. It also becomes overwhelming at the same time. It makes us laugh so damn hard that we might pee on ourselves. Have you ever had one of those "Color Purple" laughs that will remind you that all the crap that you have gone through in life is only setting you up for better? We have no option but to laugh!

I know this because like many of you reading this, I have felt every emotion that I think a human can feel. Heck, sometimes I feel like my body created new emotions. But this thing called life (ThisThingCalledLife…) as I always say to my circle of friends and family just cannot be explained; however, I do know that it can only hold you back from the enjoyment of it with your permission. This simply means that you, me, we, us make our life complicated because of secrets we do not want to share; reliving those horrible experiences; while also doing our best at trying to be perfect. We complicate our lives by living in the past. We complicate our lives because we are afraid to seek therapy, self-reflect, and be honest with ourselves. It is the ego, but until we can let our guard down and realize that it is ok that life has hurt us, that certain incidents occurred, and that we might have fallen so much that we have scars on our legs, we will never become the person we were designed to be. We must stop comparing ourselves to what society deems is most appropriate and we must be willing to live our life. What exactly does living our life mean? It simply means living for ourselves versus expecting or needing validation from outsiders who really should not have a say-so in our lives. We must also be willing to accept the scars and even those ugly bandages that we have to use sometimes. I know that no one wants to walk outside with those bandages on their arms and legs, but sometimes, in order to heal properly this is the only way to move forward. The truth is we are all imperfectly perfect and until you, me, we, us can understand this, we will always complicate our own life. No one has it all together. No one has a perfect life! Say it with me...NO ONE...HAS a PERFECT Life. Everyone is a work in progress and those with a handle on their life understand this. They are focusing on themselves, praying, and patiently pushing forward. No one has or will have a puzzle that they purchase that will be completed initially. A puzzle is designed to be put together piece by piece. And many times, we make attempts at putting the wrong pieces together and we see what happens, right? It will not fit despite how hard you push, the angle you turn it, or how frustrated you become with completing it. When it does become frustrating, we have the option to walk away and come back to it. We can walk away and return to it later with fresh eyes. We have the same option in life. This is what makes life...well interesting!

We pray to get through trials while asking why. Kind of oxymoronic, huh? When we pray, ideally, we are supposed to "Let go and let God," right? Well, because we are human and extremely inquisitive ones who desire a perfect life, we ask why and most of us are always trying to find the logic in things when the reality is: sometimes there just is not one! Many answers are simple, but we make every attempt to complicate and overthink things because we have consumed ourselves with thinking complex is better and a more suitable answer.

We pray, but also still want to be the "fixer-upper!" Ha! This defined me over the years. I have always wanted to fix people. I saw the good and I wanted to fix them, but the problem came when they didn't want to be fixed. It is part of my personality and this is a reason why we must evaluate ourselves. We must evaluate ourselves so that we can make much needed changes (and sometimes simple subtle changes), instead of entering situations with the same mind frame. We can only do so much, but for me I failed to see this, and it led me to another scar. So, this led me to a second time around divorce because when I married, I did not realize that 1. hurt, hurt; and 2. you cannot fix a person, but you can advise if they want that information. Neither are on your terms. I also had to evaluate myself because other relationships I entered; I became that same person. While it is my natural temperament, I had to work on me to grow. So, what do you have to work on and how will you get there? We realize that admitting the issue is the first step, but most of us do not understand this and many are unwilling to self-reflect because that crap hurts! It hurts to admit to self that you are not perfect. It hurts to admit to self that you might have made another mistake. But once it happens, I must say it is quite liberating.

Additionally, I learned that people ask for help, but many times people are not ready to receive help. We ask for help to assist us with those needed changes that we realize will help us, but it is oftentimes hard because change is not as easy as it seems. This has taught me to listen and just listen and never offer advice. Too often we can see the good in people, but it is not our task to make people become something that we think they should or see. People need to see their own worth and even their flaws. And honestly, both are hard. Sometimes people see the good in us when we do not see it and even when they offer such sentiments, we fail ourselves. I had a friend tell me that I was equivalent to a Lamborghini. This friend who has known we since my freshmen year in college told me how proud he was of me for all of my accomplishment. "Ki, you came from Bad Newz and look at you! You have not let life get you, and while I want you to find a mate that will work for you, you must remember that everyone cannot drive a Lamborghini without crashing. O'Shea, I am proud of you babe!" Whoa! Can you say humbling. Another friend, mentor, sister told me she knows that being in my circle is like winning the jackpot! Whoa! Another humbling comment.

So many of us have friends who see so much good in us, but until I was ready to make necessary changes to set standards and limitations on who would remain in my circle, their words were great, but were meaningless. To change, it starts from within and I had to take a moment or two or even three or four months to truly embrace myself to see this. My brother, friend told me " …it probably is extremely frustrating, but unfortunately that's the price you are going to have to pay for ambition. I can't make it seem any better. Sorry. I've tried, but truly successful people have a hard time maintaining relationships. And those degrees [that you have] are a success most people cannot imagine." So, to grow, I had to change my mind frame while praying and seriously self-reflecting. I also had to forgive myself for making poor choices and I had to stop worrying about what others thought. I even took my counselor up on blogging and sharing my story. She shared that she found me inspiring because I keep a smile on my face and even when I fall, I cry, wipe the tears and keep it moving. She said if only more people could do this, this would be most remarkable.

But it was not easy....I had to listen to the not so great comments about myself from friends. "Ki focus on you! Stop being nice because each time you are nice and allow people in, they hurt you and it's not their fault, it is yours!" One even told me that I set myself up for failure because you see the signs, but you think you are God. That hurt....no one wants to hear that it is your fault, but in order to grow, we must be willing to hear those that have a valuable opinion (now, remember everyone's opinion does not matter; as a matter of fact, you should only have a small circle to grow with and that is it).

When your loved ones share such sentiments, it causes one to feel a certain way. It might cause you pain to look at yourself a certain way, but it is great to help you grow. If your circle shed light on negative issues that everyone see that you ignore, you might want to listen so that you can grow, but it does take a special person to hear such words. Many cannot see how objective outsiders (those that matter...be careful who you listen to!) can be and when they do, it's kind of too late. But it also helps us create our own book. It helps us to walk our own path, but sometimes that path could be a lot easier if we listen and self-reflect sooner than later.

At any rate, we challenge our decisions along with those signs that we always knew were there, and even the faith that we really thought we have. I cannot give you the answer to why we do that, but I can let you know that it is not good. This thing called life is confusing, huh!? It creates chaos that seems impossible to calm. It pushes us to the edge. Don't push me cause I'm close to the edge….but seriously, it does make us feel a bit unstable at times. It makes us seem crazy, silly, dumb, and insecure, but then we have those strange moments (that should be the everyday moments) that we feel great! We feel like we are on top of the world! WE are secure in our being, in our faith, and in our decision-making process. And if only these moments lasted all of the time! They can last though if we learn to channel our energy and see that it is not the end of the world when we encounter that breakup, that manipulation from a friend, that medical diagnoses, or even that death that was unexpected. We have to remain focused and understand that we are destined to encounter such things because we human.

At eighteen years old, I thought I was grown. Nineteen years later, I wish that I was eighteen years old again only to tell my eighteen-year-old self, "Girl, girl! You have

NO dang on clue what grown really is! " Life literally is a roller coaster or my analogy is a puzzle! Those roller coasters that we love to ride at amusement parks never seem as inviting when it becomes our everyday life. From those miscarriages, to the hysterectomy's, to the abortions, to finding the loved one being unfaithful, those dips and turns and backward rides are much scarier. To seeing your loved one in a coma, to realizing that your loved one is never coming back, to that miserable breakup, we do not realize that life must still go on despite our hurt and pain. As young people, we do not even realize that those roller coaster rides become faster and faster, but while we are in the moment, we must take time to embrace and shout, and laugh, and even throw up if we need to. And once it is over, take a time to embrace it. It is ok and guess what, we typically survive them.

Recently I had a moment. Right before turning 37, I packed two suitcases after deciding to leave my now second ex-husband and moved from one country to another country. I was very mindful of who to share this journey with. There were many nosey people who were only concerned for gossip reasons. They were not like those in my circle that left me be to process, to grieve, and to pray. I had some that found out that wanted to offer their advice and pray for what they wanted. I had some that wanted to celebrate another failed marriage and was determined to comment; it must be her fault. And what I learned is, who cares. I knew what I was not going to stand for. Some would settle for what I could not bring myself to settle for. I valued myself, but I did have to be still. During this move, I really begin to juxtapose my life to a puzzle. My 36 -year -old piece of puzzle was imperfectly perfect (you will notice I love this phrase). It was filled with memories of my life; my first tape cassettes (Bobby Brown and Whitney Houston...ha! The irony); my first homecoming dance, my first boyfriend, going to college, and believe me the puzzle is not just of pictures that are all great. There are many horrible memories on that puzzle too! We will talk about those later, but this thirty-six-year-old puzzle that was filled with thousands and thousands of memories equated to so many pieces. And as I moved and had to relocate because I just couldn't stand to be in that situation anymore, I honestly felt my puzzle had come apart!

I literally broke down. I called a friend and broke down. I called another friend and broke down. I called my mentor and then another and broke down. I even found myself breaking down with my son in the car one day. At this point, I realized this: my puzzle was glued! None of those pieces were gone! Not a single one! They were all intact because the glue that held those pieces together were like that gorilla glue, but much stronger. I guess it's kinda, sorta like concrete glue. Is that such a thing? Well if not, I am a creative writer, not an expert on glue! But it is that kind of glue that will never break, tear, etc. Now, the table that my puzzle was on, it broke. Oh my, did it break. And those pieces that I had to separate into piles and wait to put them together, they fell. They were scattered. They were very scattered! Those pieces were everywhere and the only thing that was needed from me and even you is to remember that when life hits you that hard, to do what works for you. And let me preference this by saying, do what works for you; and make sure it is positive. It is hard for us to understand that it is inevitable for us to go through things. During such circumstances; death, heartaches, we must grieve. We must also reflect and figure out a way to cope. This is what therapy is for. This is what friends are for. This is what support groups are for, but so many feel as if they are too big for such groups. For me it was to pray. For me it was to go to counseling and just sit alone and reflect. Each of us process things differently. Based on my personality, it was best for me to seek counseling and find strategies to help me. I frequented the beach. I journaled, started a blog (www.thisthingcalledlifebyki.com) and I learned how to just understand that the journey was to strengthen me for my next set of obstacles. And believe me, it has helped me. It has given me a backbone that I needed. It has shown me what I need to fulfill my purpose.

For me, most did not see that I really felt scattered and it was because I had to sit still and pray alone. I constantly have people ask me how I managed to do it with a smile on my face, win teacher of the year, and still continue to move forward. I had someone who was so concerned with benefitting from me that they placed requests of things that they wanted me to purchase before I moved. They could not understand how big this new encounter I was about to embark on was for me, but instead they were only focused on what they could get from me. I had bigger things to do versus go to a store for them. I had less than two weeks to move forward and move from country. to country. I had to walk away. I had people who were afraid to share great news with me but were focused on asking me questions and it was only for gossip purposes. I had people who now call and share "I miss you," but they shared how I should remain in the situation that I needed to free myself. So, for me, it was prayer and I had to trust my discernment. I have mentors and my tight circle that prayed for me and never praying for what they wanted, but for what was meant for me. Others couldn't see this. They saw me as together. The only person that mattered that didn't see me together was myself. So, just like those extra puzzle pieces that are meaningless until you put them together, I had to remember that about my life. The puzzle is coming together quite perfectly. I was so worried about them, that I was missing the great things that were happening to me.

And this is what I have learned about ThisThingCalledLife... You must embrace it and laugh and realize that those pieces that will fall at some point will not be the detriment of you. For me, it wasn't. I still hold every great and even bad memory, my son, my circle of love, and most importantly my sanity and my faith!

So, as we begin this journey, remember ThisThingCalledLife...is not to be understood, but to find ways to enjoy it while making lasting memories that can be added to your puzzle piece.

Yours dearly,
Ki O'Shea

CHAPTER 1

Who is Kiera O'Shea?

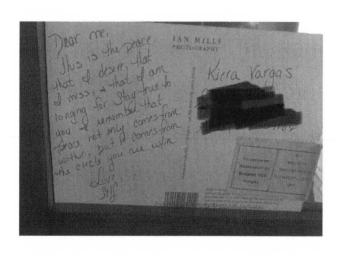

I am a naturally silly person. I love to laugh! I love to be goofy! I am extremely corny, and I can accept this about myself. I love music. I love to sing, and I don't care what ANYone says; I can! I can sing like Whitney and Jennifer! I can sing like Aretha on somedays too! Honestly, I think can blow, but in reality, I really am not that talented. However, I really don't care what people say when they hear me sing, because in my heart; in my soul; and in my mind, I can sing! YUP! I can sing!! (Ok now, I am just convincing myself....saying this as I am singing) Seriously, anything that I have ever really wanted, I have set my mind to conquer.

Even when those crazy (and I mean CRAZY....KRAZY... KKKRRRAAZZYY) obstacles appear out of nowhere I am determined to figure them out and accomplish the goals that I set. I use my resources and I do not mind asking for help. I realize that people, places, things, and ideas (I guess I could have just said nouns) are there for us to utilize. One of my favorite people (my mentor who has been there for most of my life) coined a hashtag for me #ONLYME. He always provides me with cool, motivational words and made me realize that with every bad, there really is a good, but too often we are so stuck on the bad.

I share all of the above, because I am always asked "Why are you so happy?" As a matter of fact, my sixteen-year-old son and I get this quite often. We are told that we have beautiful spirits with so much optimism. I believe it is because I know who I am. I know who I am and even when I have moments of self-doubt about life, I know the core of myself. I am comfortable singing completely out of tune. I am ok with my loud, squeaky laugh, and even in those times of doubt, deep down I know who I am, what I like, and what I will tolerate. That part of my puzzle is very clear. That confidence and assurance is that beautiful picture of myself. It was probably because of the affirmations that my parents gave me as a child. My mom would always sing a song to me, "Kiera O'Shea is her name. The prettiest little girl in the whole wide world. Kiera O'Shea is her name, is her name." And you know what? I believed it then, and I still believe it. She made me believe that about both my inner and outer beauty. She recently shared that she admires who I am. She even shared that she learns so much from me. She likes my calmness about situations and my rational thinking. We even discussed situations that have occurred when one would have been irate, but how I do not allow others to make me ugly.

My dad gave me the same assurance and made me realize the importance of education and being knowledgeable about life and what it has to offer me. This is who I am! I am smart, I am fun, I am rationale, and I am just me!

Now, although I know who I am, this does not mean that I never have moments of doubt. I do. As a matter of fact, the question of "Who is Kiera O'Shea" stems from what I should do with my last name. Oh, what shall a girl to do??! And is this stuff that we should even worry about? Well I did the other day. I went to do a craft and I had to decide what name I would add to my craft. Oh, jeezzzz what is a girl to do … I'm asking again?? Do I put my maiden name or my sons last name (my first married name) or the last name that I've had for about five years now that I've been meaning to change? I have no idea, but I do know that this is a challenge that we have, and it does take up lots of mental space. While it is so time consuming, these are things that we might battle with when trying to understand who we are. I wanted to change my last name because I thought it might make me forget those memories, but the reality of it is, it does not matter. We are ourselves! Whatever that means and for me, I prefer to spend my time elsewhere versus calling this place and that company and sending this paper in to the mortgage company and of course having to pay for that passport that I just got. and what about the cars?? Is it worth it? Does my last name define me? I thought so! I didn't just think so, I was adamant about changing it, but now I just don't know...I'm Kiera! I'm Kiera O'SHEA.

I still have the same social security number. I was born at the same location. I still have the same past memories. I still have the same chicken pox scar and the same scar on my leg from that darn oven. I still have the same parents, the same sister, the same child, the same everything. I'm overall the same person with new lessons and reminders that everything that we do serves a purpose. I am also the same person that will continue to make dumb choices sometimes. I will always fall short of being perfect, but I will grow from each mistake. I have learned to be vulnerable. This was hard for me. It was hard for me to learn the importance of vulnerability. I have learned the importance of life. I have also learned the importance of building a circle that works for me. I laugh as I say this, but I have also realized that the only validation that I need is me. So many focus and center on what others think about them. Now, again, we do need those in our inner circle to help us so that we can grow, but we know what changes are needed in most cases. Many use social media to measure their lives and even create goals, and while I have never been that person, my journey has truly taught me to enjoy **my** life. Laugh alone. Laugh with genuine people. Trust my gut. Hug my son tighter. Take as many trips as I want solo. Go to concerts alone. Tell a person when they are wrong. If they walk away, so what. Don't apologize when someone hurts you. Be happy and don't try to hide your emotions. Chase your goals. Don't wait for others to go to the movie with you. Don't allow people to take up your time with negativity. Don't settle. Don't allow anyone to manipulate you. Don't share if you don't desire. Dance with my dog. Take long walks. Say no and do not do things that serve no importance to me. Overall, be true to you! This is a hard concept for so many.

This reminds me of other things that we think about that do not serve much relevance to our lives. We think so much about things. And it's important to think things through, but sometimes we allow things to keep our center focus versus focusing on things that could assist us with bettering ourselves; hence, exercise or starting that business. I can definitely attest to this. To help myself stay focused, I started creating exercises for myself and creating things that I want to do for myself. I also started completing those tasks. I wanted to start kickboxing, so I signed up for a class. The class has turned into a year membership and while I hurt, it feels good. I always wanted to travel to Jerusalem, so I took a trip with a friend there. I was excited to write a book, so I sat down and wrote. To grow and to accomplish your purpose, you have to be willing to do it.

Throughout this book, you will have tasks to complete. Take time to complete them to assist you with becoming who you were meant to be.

#ThisThingCalledLife Task #1-

As you focus on your day today, tomorrow, and in the future, think about what's important. Make a list of things that you find to be important!

CHAPTER 2

When in Doubt, Find the Confidence That Lives in You!

I am sure that I passed confidence, assurance, and the importance of education to my son. When I asked him one day how does he cope while being a Type 1 diabetic, the many transitions that he has endured, and even the most devastating one; being in a coma for almost a week, with doctors believing he would be brain dead, he smiled and shrugged and said "I just do it." While this example does not define confidence, but faith, I assure you my son is confident that everything happens the way it is to happen. He walks in a room with colorful socks, a loud neon shirt, and he could care less what anyone thinks of him. This is important. This is important because so many care what others think. We were fortunately to go to school together (I taught at both schools his freshmen and sophomore years of high school and I am optimistic and believe that he enjoyed us being together every day) during his first two years of high school. Students constantly came up and shared with me how they liked his outfits. His "fits" as they called it were nice. I was blown because I felt he looked a mess some days with those loud colors and colors that I didn't necessarily think went together. Fortunately, he is confident in himself and he has never been a follower. He is always the leader of the back. His story, his confidence is what I see many lack.

I have watched people take the same picture over ten and twelve times. The pictures come out the same, but one commented, "If I am going to post, I have to make sure no one saw that piece of hair." Very interesting because it shows the picture is not even about the person, but about those looking at the picture. To grow, we must focus on ourselves. What others have to think should not matter, yet it does.

This is how easy it is to live your life. Remember those puzzle pieces we continue to reference? Well, the easy part of life is those outside pieces. When you know what makes you, you, (slow down and read that...When you know what makes YOU, YOU...take that in!) that is the foundation of your puzzle. That is the foundation of you. If you are anything like me, those are the pieces that you start with when you begin your puzzle. They are easy. They are easy because you don't have to stress out about who you are. Knowing who you are, what you like, and what you want in life are the essential pieces of your puzzle.

Individuals must focus on what matters to them. I took trips solo when others made excuses. I walked on the beach alone when others stayed in the hotel applying make up for others. I am confident in the mistakes and choices that I made and could care less what others think. I share my testimony despite what others think because I have come to realize that my journey has inspired others. This was evident recently when I listened unintentionally to two women sharing a horrible circumstance. I tried to ignore, but I was pushed to say something, mail cards to them, and I recently received feedback from them sharing they were thankful. I share my journey with many and while I think it was what I was supposed to do, many are unsure how to make the first step to make changes, so remember your journey is important for a reason. My journey and your journey are meant to be shared so that we can embrace life and offer our young people the encouragement that they need. To do that, we have to show them that regardless of what is going on, what has happened, we can conquer all of our dreams. We have to also remind them that life is not over if they make mistakes. We must teach them to have confidence and to listen to their gut. While we are teaching them this, we must teach them to have confidence and to do that, we as adults must have confidence.

They are the essential pieces to understanding ThisThingCalledLife... Those pieces are less complicated, and they help with the organization of your puzzle. That is similar to life. Even those bad and scary parts of life are easy for us to deal with, because they are just small reminders that the entire puzzle cannot be hard! If you know who you are, you can have a lot more control over those complications.

#ThisThingCalledLife Task #2-

In this chapter, I challenge you to come up with a list of things that you are truly sure of about yourself! What do you like? What do you dislike? Let's begin this puzzle and start with that border; this is the easy part! And as you come up with this list, be reminded that these are those pieces that will forever help you conquer!

$\mathcal{C}$HAPTER 3

Is Your Circle #Dope? If Not, You Should Find #DopeFriends

Did you complete your assignment? Look at the previous chapters to check your assignments. Did you create a list to help you learn who you are? Did you create a list of things you like and dislike? Did you create things that you are interested in completing during your lifetime? Whoa, I really do sound like a teacher, but this is what was asked of me when I decided to write this book. All of the above is that foundation to that puzzle that I continue to reference. This is the easy stuff. Most of us know what we like and dislike, even if we are afraid to admit it. Most of us know what we want to do, even if we make every excuse in the world to avoid completing it. I love music as mentioned before. Music keeps me motivated and when I need that extra push, I prescribe myself the music that I need at that time. Whether trap music, gospel music (don't judge me...) or some R&B slow jams, music is something I must have. Therefore, music and other things are my foundational pieces. They are the pieces that I can put together without hesitation.

I know this about me. I've answered those questions, have you? So, when my storm comes, I am prepared. I also love to write. I blog, I journal, I write letters to myself.

I have had several people over the last few months ask me how I was able to conquer so much in my young life. I was initially flattered by the term young, but I couldn't really answer the question because I don't really know. I do know that: I stick with what I start. I don't give up. I pray A LOT! I believe in me and when it seems as if I will never find that puzzle piece, I sit back for a moment and just relax. I realize that life happens, but I also realize that excuses are just that. And outside of that, I just have amazing people in my life. I keep positive people in my life, and I am quick to eliminate people full of drama or those that cannot add to my life. Seems selfish? Well, it is true. I need people, just like you need people in your life that will uplift me, help me grow, and will provided me with the constructive criticism that I need when I am not being my best self. So, this is another piece of my puzzle.

I blog about people that inspire me. I have taken those that have given me some sort of encouragement and I have shared their stories. I have shared the successes of men. I have shared the challenges that women face. I have even shared stories of hardships that I have gone through because our stories motivate and uplift many.

I have cards and text messages. I hold dear to memories. I take pictures, but I prefer to be in the moment when I am engaging with people. My journaling helps me to reflect. It allows me to reflect on how I can grow and be better. For example, I journaled about an argument I had with a loved one recently. I was able to read what I wrote a few days later and see that I failed to be objective. I was able to go back and see how the entire argument could have been fixed if things were done differently. And I learned this technique by incorporating what my circle has done to assist them with being better people.

I have a best friend who is truly optimistic, and they have a "God-box." They write things in that box and stick it in their and walk away. I could never understand how they just let things go, but they taught me how to have more faith and such people are those that you want in your circle. Often, we have people that call us to socialize and to do things, but when or how many people do you have in this day and age that you can really connect with without using technology? I know I can, but can you? I have learned to do this, and I went even further and created a thank you jar. And when I have been in my feelings, I have taken moments to write out what I am thankful for to take my mind off of my worries. My "thank you's" are everything from: my career, my dog, my son, my vision, my health. We sometimes take such things for granted. But a friend of mine reminded me never to accept anything and always believe that we can conquer the desires of our heart. I realized it is giving thanks to what we already have.

I hold my friends near and dear to me, so I take time to spend quality time with them. I listen, they listen. We actively engage in doing things that we like together.

This helps us bond more and it also helps when I do have problems because I know that my friends will actively listen and offer even the harshest criticism if that means making me better and stronger. Having such friendships are essential to growing.

I recently had someone share that they never had a friendship circle like mine. That is fine, but everyone needs people in their life that will uplift them. They need people that will tell them the hard truth. They need those people that will motivate them when they fall (because we all fall). They need people that will also bandage them up when they fall. And they need to reciprocate this because friendship is not one-sided.

This is why I share with people that outside of Oprah and Ice Cube (I just love them two...Ice Cube because we share a name), I do not want any new friends. My friends and I have grown together. We have pulled out tissue for each other. We have had those ugly cries together, while making each other laugh at the same time. We have learned how to accept the constructive criticism and those passive aggressive acts of love. We share photos of our happy moments. We are happy for our friends even if we are not always feeling our best. We take moments to send a simple text or take a selfie to make sure even when we are having a good moment, we need to check on the friend that might be down. We are unafraid to share secrets because we do not judge. We have no intentions of harming and in an instant, we will stop the whole world for our friend. We understand that if one does not answer the phone, that they are busy, and this does not upset us. My friends are MVP's and every time I think of the love, respect, and support that we give to each other; I know I am blessed.

What I was told and what I believe is this: Your friends are you. So, I shared with students one day: If you look at your friends and you shake your head sad at their actions, they are you. Find friends who can make you better, who you are not embarrassed to be like, and that you can hold conversations with; not just texts and fake selfies.

#ThisThingCalledLife Task #3

Make a list of people who assist with uplifting you, helping you flourish. In addition, write down things that you have learned from them and how they have helped you become a better you.

CHAPTER 4

#FocusMan

After that storm settles, I am always shocked at how much I have accomplished, but the key is to stay focused. Stay in your zone. Find something to keep you in that zone. Follow what Tupac says, "Keep yo head up....things will get brighter.." The only answer any of us can give to such a question is: we follow our hearts even through those crazy storms. The stillness of the after effect of the storm is comforting ONLY because we know it is the end; no more damages, but now it is time to clean up, and figure out how to pick up those pieces. Please note, I am not trying to make light of our world catastrophes.

I write letters to myself. I also write letters to people. I write letters in my journals as therapy for myself. I wrote to myself awhile back. The letter was after I met a woman on a solo trip I took. She was so amazed that I was taking a solo trip. It amazed her more that the trip was not the first solo trip that I had taken. She was so shocked, and she promised herself during our conversation that she would do more for herself. She was in her sixties and she regretted never doing anything for herself. She waited on people, she made excuses, she accepted things that she now regrets, and as she shared, I listened, while making a promise to myself that I will continue to enjoy life with no regrets as long as I could help it. I listened to her as she described just how her choices caused her to miss out on things that she always wanted to do, but now at sixty-two she felt limited. She couldn't go back in time and just listening to her was one of those learning lessons that we can never receive from a textbook. I enjoy listening to people and meeting people. The encounters that I have, we will discuss here. The stories that I have listened to provide me with wisdom and just an appreciation for life. #listeningtorandomstories #wisdom #thisthingcalledlife #choicesarekeyinLife

After meeting her, I continued to look at the waves, and prayed that she would be able to conquer her fears and just enjoy life! Remember there is no such thing as perfect, but we all are imperfectly perfect people. I prayed that she was able to accomplish things on her list and let go of all of the things that were preventing her from being unhappy. Life does that to us. As I mentioned before I always feel the need to help, and even here I was helping a total stranger when I was just sitting alone looking at the waves. Just by listening to her, I might have helped her, but she helped me too. She made me realize the importance of living life regardless of the storms that we are faced with in life. In life we need those foundational pieces, because they are easy for us to put together. Those pieces are who they are. For me: I am a natural helper. I am spiritual. I am a learner. I love my solitude. I love traveling alone. I love being with great people. I love socializing and listening to people stories. I am extremely reflective. I am learning how to forgive. I am learning how to accept life's imperfections.

With that, here is that letter that I wrote to myself after that encounter:

Dear Ki,

Can you believe how much you have grown over the years? I am reading old journals that you wrote, and my heart is so happy for you! Girl!! You are doing great things! I am proud of you! Do not ever take what you do lightly! You are phenomenal and I am proud of you because you have achieved great accomplishments while being your true self. With all of the mistakes you have made, you are learning. You are learning that there is no secret to life. In in the midst of storms and heartaches and just being unsure, you survived girl! With the many many many (did I say MANY) mistakes that you have made and poor choices that you have made, keep learning from them. Don't keep making the same mistakes over because then I might have to talk about you. (YUP! I said it!) Your dad called a few days ago and it was quite surprising to hear him say, "You really exceeded my expectations of you. I knew you would do great, but you did so much more and you should always be proud of yourself. You are touching lives and allowing others to touch your lives and that is important." Many people will never have those remarks made by their parents and that comment alone had to touch you.

Remember that no one is perfect and despite what you have gone through, you are an amazing woman who has exceeded what many will conquer. You are also healing. You will always be in healing mode because this is what growing looks like. We grow by being delivered from those challenging circumstances that we encounter. You are a victor and you must focus on the good in every situation that you go through. That storm is bound to happen. Without the storm or the rain, we would constantly have dry soil (hmmmmmm I cannot find an analogy for that, but just know it would not be good to always have everything work in your favor). You are special. You are kind and loving. You are transparent and humble. You will continue to reap what you are supposed to sow because you are following your path. You have no reason to listen to any outside voices, so keep being patient. Keep finding the good. Continue to love yourself and never sell yourself short.

Forgive yourself. It is ok to make small or big mistakes. They are all the same. As long as you learn, that is the secret to growth. As you learn, make needed changes. If that means, weeding people out of your life, do that. If that means placing a check beside something that you have wanted to do, that is what you need to do. Grow and flourish and be happy! Protect yourself, while following your dream.

Continue dating yourself and praying for your Boaz. Continue being a great mom and praying for other things that you desire. Be happy with what you have and overall love you!

Remember that trip you went on solo? Remember that older woman who shared she admired you for taking trips alone? Well, make sure this is something you add to that puzzle. Each encounter that you have with someone may be a piece of wisdom that you need to help you in #ThisThingCalled life... But think of what she shared with you. Don't forget to be you and enjoy every moment even when it gets hard. This is who you are Ki. You are a goal-setter. You are fearless and you are greatness in the making! Keep enjoying life, reflecting on ways to make you better, and most importantly learning from your mistakes."

Love your favorite gal,

Ki' O'Shea

#ThisThingCalledLife- Task 4

With that being said, take the time to write a letter to yourself! Give yourself kudos and think about a recent encounter that you have had with a person that has helped you learn more about yourself.

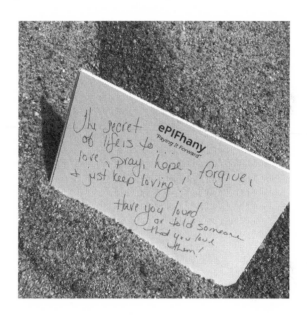

CHAPTER 5

Love Yourself and Believe You Are Awesome

I shared something with a good friend, and she gave me the above title. She also said, "you are so awesome." I think the same about her. She is a beautiful person inside and out and has been through so many of my trials with me. She has also provided me joy. I remember this one time we took a road trip, and although it was not funny then, but her tire burst. The story ended with her running into the arms of a homeless man. We laughed about this and so many things on a seriously impromptu trip to out of the country. When we lived abroad, we would talk just about every morning for hours and laugh and share insight on so many things. We talked about life. We shared lots of intimate stories and we would always uplift each other. We are both exceptions to the rules of #thisthingcalledlife. Life is so much better with great people, and she exemplifies what a true friend is. She teaches me still how to always love myself and admit the flaws that we all have.

We co-host a This Thing Called Life podcast together and on our first episode, she shares a story about me and my not so great actions. I recall that time and when we do encounter those times that were not so great, we have to remember that despite…we are still awesome!

During a church sermon, I watched a sister and a brother share love. The sister, who was about four or five years old kept reaching over trying to kiss her brother. She giggled each time. It was so adorable. She tried to grab his cheeks, and he kept pulling away giggling as well. When she finally got to kiss him, they giggled so hard. And at this time, he stopped pretending he did not want the kiss, and he also hugged and kissed her back. He was about seven years old. Their other brother who was near their age watched with fascination, adoration, and also smiled so hard.

To be an exception to any rule, you must know and understand love. You must have a genuine circle of love who will allow you to pour out your heart and pour out laughter. This is me and so many of you readers. I am always reminded that my light shines so bright and it is because I understand love and how we are supposed to pass this love forward all of the time. As a matter of fact, I was told to sit down and truly embrace my greatness.

A letter that I received once shared "..."has really shown me more and more how "one of a kind" you are. The letter also shared "your perspective on life and its twist and turns is nothing short than amazing." To be an exception, you must understand that life is definitely a game that we have control over. As hard as it is, you and I can always conquer, but it is hard, because we do not always see the great potential that we have. We fail to realize that our flaws help us, and they will not mess up our puzzles.

Even as people remind us of our greatness,, we sometimes have a hard time acknowledging it because of self-doubt or those moment . For me it was because I did not really see myself as a standout, but with each of those amazing people in my life, I can now understand, embrace, and see my greatness. A card reads "Thank you for letting me be your friend. You are truly a gift to me and to the world; I wish that you could see what I see when I look at you. Because you are so selfless and are constantly doing for other people, here is a small note..." I had to believe that I was greatness to be greatness. I had to reflect on the words of my mentors, mentees, friends, and even family members who have spoken greatness over me. To be able to see yourself as greatness, you have to have those people in your life that are confident, that are dope, and that are also amazing.

To be exception, it is about having people in your corner to remind you of this. Even the strongest person needs this reminder sometimes and this is why I keep cards and letters because they are playbacks of when I need that extra push. So, I am an exception to the rule. You are an exception to the rule. Say it loud... "I am an exception to the rule! Say it once more!

About few years ago, I endured a pretty hopeless marriage. I gave up so much of my materialistic items, but the love that I was shown was far more rewarding. This was another example of me being an exception. We have the capabilities to conquer fearful tasks, but only if we allow love in our hearts, and we pour love into others. Love is the solution to everything in my mind, heart, and soul.

While writing over the last year, I had a good friend send me a text to share his current whereabouts. He has just been admitted to the hospital and will be in there for a while. I immediately asked if I could call, and as we chatted, I sent up prayers (God bless this young person. Hold him up and allow him to believe in the miracle that is coming his way. You can fix anything. You are the miracle worker...). I can still recall this young person taking the time to help me apply to law school. I recall an even more recent time that he dropped what he was doing at midnight to make a phone call for me to assist another person. Even while in pain, he helped. Exceptions to the rules are only because love is involved. He is also an exception to the rule! His testimony, his faith, and his ability to love even as he experiences hardships amazes me! He constantly updates me on his health, and I send loud and silent prayers for him. He has no idea how much he inspires me.

I have another friend that listens to me intently. I can only imagine what goes on in his head, but he always pushes me to be better. When I feel as if it gets hard or that I just don't want to do it, his always silly, fun personality is turned into a more serious, nurturing, brotherly tone to remind me never to quit. Those are the amazing people in my circle.

I am constantly receiving random texts, pictures, and facetime messages sharing great news and asking if I am ok. I receive prayers and true genuine love and that makes a difference. Whether I am having a great day already or if I am having a pretty long tedious day, those messages are amazing! And to ensure that I am fulfilling my purpose, I pass them forward. I love those that love me, and I even share words of affirmation with people who cross my mind.

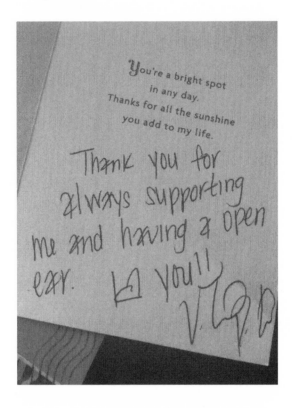

A few months ago, a sorority sister invited me to dinner. She shared God told her to contact me. We knew each other and have always been cordial, but she took the time to listen. She shared her story with me and allowed me to see that she was coming from a genuine place. We ate dinner, I listened, and I realized she was sent to me to help me with the circumstances I had encountered. She took the time to reach out to me because I was in her thoughts. Not everyone will do this, and I am a firm believer that people enter our thoughts for particular reasons.

So, how does these stories tie into the title? An exception to the rule is being loved so deeply, passing on that love with no hesitation, and understanding that in order to grow, you must have great people to uplift you! To be an exception, you must also believe that you are greatness. You must exhibit humility. You must genuinely give back. Being an exception is not hard, but it does require work. Being an exception also requires you to take moments to forgive yourself and even look at your flaws. How can your flaws help you to become a better person? Are you willing to be that exception?

#ThisThingCalledLife Task #5

I challenge each reader to comment and share why you are an exception to the rule! Think of how the flaws that you have are helping you to help others? We all are exceptions, so brag about your exceptions and embrace #ThisThingCalledLife....We Are ALL Exceptions to the rule!

CHAPTER 6

Being Vulnerable for Yourself

I have realized that many people are unaware of their true worth. They settle for mediocre and/or people who cannot assist them growing to be that beautiful flower. I can attest to allowing mediocre despite what others have seen in me. I had to have a talk with myself about this issue. This contradicted everything that I saw in myself. I mean, I love myself, I treat myself to trips and dinners and I even have a #dopeCircle, but sometimes we truly do settle for less than what we deserve. I typically send out cards to people when I think of them. In these cards I write meaning, heartfelt things. One of your assignments were to write a letter to yourself. The problem with writing to yourself versus others for me is being truly vulnerable to myself. It was hard to truly allow myself to see my flaws. You know the flaws that we just spoke about. It was also hard for me to admit that I allowed people to do certain things to me because I was too nice, and I also didn't see my true worth sometimes.

I visited a nail shop a few days ago. I didn't need to go, but to waste time and obviously money, I went. I sat beside a beautiful woman who was on the phone. While I assumed it was a man that she was with, and that assumption was right, I heard myself. I heard her pleading and selling herself to this guy. I opened up my phone to my blog app and went to one of my posts and asked her to read it. She looked at me and we had a nice discussion about it. Sometimes we have to admit why things go wrong. We often let people and even work, or anything come into our lives and treat us with no respect. We continuously allow it and to get over it, we have to be willing to be honest with ourselves, which means being vulnerable.

I realized that what I have gone through many would not be able to let go and truly embrace what life has offer. In order for me to embrace this, I had to block out what I thought others would have to say about me. I had to block out those moments of self-doubt. I had to open my heart and allow myself to be vulnerable. This vulnerability had nothing to do with others, but I had to be vulnerable for myself. Oftentimes one fails to see how happy they can be just by being alone and learning themselves. This allows one to know their own worth.

If you don't take the time to know yourself and embrace yourself, how do you expect another person to do so? If I didn't know my worth, I would fall back into the same cycle I came from; dealing with the same things I dealt with, but we have a choice to be happy! Happiness stems from so many things; joy, self-reflection, being true to you. Happiness also stems from being able to truly let go of the past, unless of course you are ONLY using it as a method to grow and become a better you. To do this, you must be vulnerable.

And each time I felt I was falling short of being the person that I was, I had to remind myself to do better. I had to figure out things to help myself so that I would remember that I am only a vulnerable human trying to be better than I have been. I work on a college campus and daily I see a young person in a wheelchair. They wheel themselves to class daily. I have yet to be close to the person, but I stand watching and just seeing the strength and the perseverance that they must have to wake up and do this daily. We all hold things that are hard for us, but it is all on how we push ourselves to that next place. Daily this young person pushes themselves to class, to eat, etc. This is something that we all should keep in mind. Our issues are only as big as we make them. We only have to wake up and push ourselves to the next point. Are you doing this?

We are all beautiful flowers in our flowerbeds. They are all so beautiful, but sometimes you meet people who never took care of their flowerbeds. These people have weeds in their beds that are camouflaged as flowers. We overlook weeds sometimes. I did once before, and I was certain this green thing in my yard was a flower until I looked closer and even had someone come look at it with me. I was convinced this "beautiful" thing was a flower, but it was definitely a weed.

This becomes problematic because if you do not know your worth, the worth of your precious flower beds, then this results in you allowing someone in your flower bed who will destroy your flowers with their weeds. Weeds can be symbolic of anything; bringing down your self-esteem, verbal abuse, physical abuse, manipulation, neglecting self, and so much more.

I've finally slowed myself down to pay more attention to those that I give a seat to on my patio because I cannot risk them dropping one of their seeds... I mean weeds into my flower bed and destroying the beauty of what I've worked so hard to maintain. Everyone has flowers in the background of their puzzles. Be sure not to mistake a weed for one.

So, as you work on being happy and healthy, be mindful of who you allow near your flowers...

Protect you...and find someone that enhances your flowerbed!

#ThisThingCalledLife – Task 6

Take a moment to be vulnerable with self. This could be anything; for example, a walk in a park, drinking a cup of coffee alone, going to a grave site to visit a loved one. Take a moment to identify the weeds that you might have in your life. Once you do this, continue to the next chapter.

CHAPTER 7

Hold Yourself on a Pedestal

Life is not complicated. We make it hard. We select our battles. We allow people to treat us in ways that are unhealthy. We follow the unhealthy footsteps of our past; whether it is stemmed from our families or our grown-up personal experiences. We give too much trust to people even when we do feel in our gut that it is not right. I believe in forgiving, but oftentimes we still try to force a puzzle piece when we should break ties with that person or things. We know when we are unhealthy.

We hold people on pedestals, but fail to hold ourselves on pedestals? I wonder why? Is it because of that self-doubt we discussed earlier? Is it because we are still trying to learn how to love ourselves? Or is it because we really think people are better than us? I don't know about you, but I remind myself daily of how amazing I am. I am amazing and as mentioned, I don't always see all of my potential, but I am learning. We all fail to give ourselves the credit that we deserve. This is another essential part of growing in life!

If you do not think you are amazing or worthy of things, no one else will. It is not about selling yourself to people, but it is about realizing yourself worth! I believe that we have gifts. I believe that we know the path that we should take even if we stray off a bit. I know that we are aware when those puzzle pieces are not pieces that should be in our box (those "friends" are NOT your friends...JayZ and Bey said "...no foes;" that workplace is not where you should be, but it's easy ....right...).

I always tell people how amazing they are. It's my favorite word of affirmation. I watch people and I am inspired by many. I am inspired by the friend who gets promoted. I am inspired by the friend who battles medical issues. I am inspired by the friend who just opened a business. I am inspired by that one person who does great on a test. I am inspired by that friend who had an emergency surgery and is always so positive. People are amazing. We are astonishing creatures. We are impressive! As creepy as it sounds, I like to people watch. I watch parents with their children. I watch couples walk hand in hand. I watch teachers teach their classrooms. I watch administrative assists help customers in their windows.

We are amazing creatures and we fail to give ourselves the treats that we deserve.

To do this it's a balancing act and we have to take a moment to catch our rhythm sometimes. How many of you have ever double-dutch before? When you are getting your rhythm to jump in between both of those ropes, we bop, we move our shoulders, we tap or feet, we hear music, but when we get into that rope, we maintain that rhythm..for a while anyway, and then what do we do? We do it again. We rock, we count aloud, we sing chants, the friends that are turning the ropes for us help us and to know how amazing you are, you need them to chant as you find your rhythm and jump in your ropes. And when you lose that beat, find it again. It may be to another chant, it might even be to new friends turning this time (you know when the street lights came on, some had to run home, so they put those ropes down...), but you can do it because you are amazing!

There is no better way to describe our bravery as we walk the path of our particular circumstance. We all have a story. We all are defeaters of that dragon that is in our lives. We all are the heroes and sheros in our story book, but we fail to see this. We worship people when we should take the time to worship ourselves. Think of the testimony that you have. Oftentimes we don't believe that we did anything great. Well for me, I was reminded how I drove 75 miles one way to get to law school. I was reminded of the classes I taught while doing this. I was reminded of watching my son fight for his life while he was in a coma. I was reminded of my childhood and even my young adulthood circumstances. And I have a testimony that people actually "awe" over. I don't even put myself on a pedestal, but others see me as having to accomplish what others never could. But if we are on our path, we all have a testimony. When we don't always feel our amazingness, then we need people to remind us. We all lose ourselves and that is when we need those reminders. Those reminders that we should be placed on a pedestal. Whether it is accomplishing something like running your first 5k or completing medical school after being on academic suspension during your undergraduate years, you have conquered and should hold your head up high and pat yourself on your back.

I am a firm believer that we are all Biblical characters. We are the Martha's. We are the Jonah's. We are Hagar and even Daniel. We are given tasks to complete and each task is filled with many things to help us complete our puzzles. I found this article that I was planning to send to "Modern Love" that I wrote in August 2017 and it reminded me of my strength. In four years, I have moved four times. From city to city; country to country, state to state, I have put a lot of miles on me and I applaud myself and deem myself as amazing.

Prior to that I was growing and being praised. Prior to that I was working several jobs to build my resume, while working on my first master's degree. Before that, I was doing something amazing, and before that I was also doing other amazing things while facing challenges. Each journey forced me to wipe those tears, tie my boots up (I prefer heels, so gracefully slide in those heels) and walk with grace. And I have learned that we need to celebrate all of our victories and we need to humbly stand on our own pedestal.

#ThisThingCalledLife -Task #7

I wrote a letter that I later uploaded to my blog that sheds light on my amazingness. I challenge you to take a moment to either share a story or write it in privacy about your amazing moment. This moment could be one that might have been filled with lots of emotions but have helped you to find those correct puzzle pieces.

Mine has helped me accept all of the greatness that HE is bringing into my life and has shown me just how #DOPE and #Amazing I am.

Be good to you and applaud yourself for how amazing you are!

CHAPTER 8

Relax, Drink Tea, and Learn to Embrace It All

I believe my first massage was in my early twenties. I still get them, because if I didn't, I might just lose my mind. This is one of the many consistent things that I do. I pamper myself by doing things for myself. For me, this is what I need to ensure I allow those daily stressors of life to escape my body. I also take care of my nails, my hair, and my mind. I go to therapy when I need it. I call a friend if I need to just talk. I take walks. I sit on the beach. And then there are times when I just drink tea. I drink tea and as I blogged before, I have imagined having tea with Oprah. We will sit over tea and just discuss life. We will come to a consensus about the difficulties of life, but I'm sure we will agree with….

Life is as complicated as we make it. I am in no way saying that doing the above prevents me from stressing or even prevents me from thinking of those bills that are always there, those low days that I have had, or even the challenges of my everyday life. What I am saying is that by taking care of you and learning to be still and allowing your body, mind, and soul to relax, you will feel a bit better. Many people do not know how to relax. I remember reading somewhere that many are afraid of being in a room alone. Many are afraid to sit at a restaurant alone or even in their rooms without the television on because silence scares people. It allows them to hear the sounds of their own minds and the sounds of whatever other sounds a person might hear. Many have yet to take a vacation alone. Many are afraid to make that step for various reasons; safety, fear, but in order to appreciate yourself and learn yourself, it is essential that we all do this.

In my silent moments, I hear God pushing me in the direction that I am supposed to move. I hear a peace that reminds me of just how great life can be when you embrace the crazy, insane, sorrow, love, happiness, and indifferent in your life. Daily, we have puzzle pieces thrown into our boxes. These pieces are the chaos of life and many of these pieces do not belong in our box, but we keep them. We keep them because we are afraid that we will not have enough pieces to complete our puzzles versus embracing the fact that all of those darn pieces are not meant to be in our box. We can look at the shape, the colors, and we can immediately tell they are not part of our puzzle, but we hold on to them. And we are filling our box with pieces that need to be disposed. They are just there and are serving no point; for example, people, materialistic items, more people... can you think of something in your life that you can rid yourself of now?

When we do this, we prevent ourselves from experiencing peace. We can never relax when we feel that negativity surround us. I remember becoming so tense and anxious when I would hear a certain car or certain footsteps. That is not healthy. I knew I was supposed to be somewhere else, but I was greedy, and I wanted to be overly prepared for my puzzle. Just what if that piece was needed later? And the reality is, it was truly evident that the puzzle piece did not belong to me. To be healthy is being cognizant of your peace and surroundings. Healthy is knowing when to walk away from those loud screams, that person that continues to grab on to your coat tail and blocking out the deadly sounds of chaos that. To obtain peace and learn to relax, it starts with listening to your body. It starts with just sitting and meditating and just bring in the moment. How many can sit in the dark and just relax? How many can cut the tv or remove their fingers from their cell phones (yeah, I said it right…)? How many can take a long walk without wondering who posted on social media? How many people are comfortable with shutting down their cell phones at night? These are things that will assist you with being still and being in the moment.

I laugh when I watch people take pictures of everything! I love pictures and one of my travel buddies will tell you I take pictures of random things (I blogged and wrote about that too). But some that have never gone anywhere fail to be in the moment because they are tied to recording everything. Just sit, be still, and appreciate the sun. Look to your right and take in the sights. Look to the left and watch the people. Breathe deep. Listen to the sounds. Take it in and this will do a lot of good for your soul!

We must learn to embrace our space. We must learn to love ourselves so much that we can sit alone in the light or dark. We must embrace ourselves and be comfortable with allowing those stresses to fall off of you.

Be still and grab a cup of tea and be at peace.

#ThisThingCalledLife -Task #8

What is the hardest thing for you to do alone? Why is this? Are you afraid to go to the movies alone? Are you afraid to take a trip solo? Are you afraid to just sit in your home with no electronics? Take a moment to answer the first question. Now, over the next few days, if it is feasible try to figure out why the task is hard for you to do it alone. Plan to try this in the next day, week, month, or year.

CHAPTER 9

I Put Stickies on Everything

When my son was in second grade, I walked into his bathroom and I saw a sticky note that he wrote himself. The note read, "Be good at math." He has never been much of a math person, and to be honest neither have I. I can make every excuse as to why, but that is really not the point that I am making here. He wrote a sticky note to himself. It was yellow and it was on his bathroom mirror. I had this sense of pride on this day. He mirrored what he saw me do. I write in expo makers on my mirrors. I play tic-tac-toe with him on our bathroom mirror. I make smiley faces on my mirrors. I write out goals and visions for myself on my mirrors. And when I look at myself in these mirrors, I see my goals. Currently I see " Life is a roller coaster, a marathon, and a complicated story, but everything is possible" on my mirror. I also see "Keep focusing! Continue listening and everything is possible." I have other goals on my mirror. I have dates that I will accomplish the goals. I have several different areas that I want to improve.

For as long as I can remember I have written down my goals. I did this before I picked up my first self-help book. I remember my sophomore year of high school when I sat down and wrote out the days and weeks that I had left before I left my hometown. I knew how many days I had until graduation with weekends and how many days I had until graduation without weekends. I wrote out my goals, which were not really much at the time. I wanted to be successful.

I visit my friend and when I leave their homes with sticky notes everywhere! I leave notes everywhere. I leave them words and prayers of affirmations. I do the same for myself because I must remind myself of goals. I must see them. I must visualize and to do this, you have to write them down.

I wonder if I even accomplished that goal. What does successful mean? I used to believe that it meant having degrees and having a high paying job, but I am sure that is not what it means to me anymore. Successful means being happy with self. Successful means being happy and content. It means setting goals that make you happy. My son wants to be an artist. I know he was probably a bit nervous when we first talked about college. I know he was even nervous about bringing math test grades home, but he has now learned that I want him to be happy in whatever he does.

In order to be happy, we must set goals for ourselves. You can be like me and write them all over your mirror. You can put sticky notes all over the house like I do with positive affirmations, or you can just stick them in your wallet. I am a firm believer that you must have those goals close to you. You must be able to see them and remind yourself of those goals when life feels like it is tumbling down. My goals are now to be a better me. My goals center around being around like-minded people who have loving intentions. I create new goals often. It does not have to be at the beginning of the year. It does not have to be on my birthday. Whenever I feel the need to set new goals, I set them.

Being happy means being true to your visions. It means refraining from trying to walk into someone else's jungle or steal another person's puzzle piece. Being happy means taking ownership of your life versus allowing others to manage your life. In 2019, we are so hooked to technology and social media that we have a false ideal of what success and accomplishment looks like. We desire fake personas, and many have no idea who they are because they are always adding more and more to themselves because they are unhappy with self. If you are unhappy with self, being able to accomplish your goals will be a difficult task.

While I have always been a visual person who loves to journal, my son is completely opposite of me. His peace and his love are drawing. While we both love music, we have our own favorites. While we both love our peace, we have different ideals of what we do to retrieve that peace. I sit in complete solitude, but he sits with a pencil and a sketchbook.

Over the last few months, I have gone through crates of cards and letters. I have so many of them from all stages of my life. I came across quotes that I wrote down. I came across my thoughts in journals. I came across pieces that I wrote. I can across news paper articles.

I even came across an old planner and I am currently working with the company that I wanted two years ago. I am happy. Even with my challenges, I am happy. And my happiness stems from seeing that life happened, but I did not let it break me. Those around me that are experiencing life; sickness, divorces, new jobs, loss of loved ones, miscarriages, etc. are my inspiration...

we all know that #ThisThingCalledLife is as hard and complicated as you make it

Some things are inevitable, and we must be able to be optimistic while walking through #ThisThingCalledLife. If you are anything like me, when you accomplish your goals, you feel that sense of accomplishment and can breathe. You can now envision your next step. But to do this, you must be comfortable in your own skin. To do this, you must be able be in your happy place. I recently sat back and looked at all that I have accomplished, been through, and seen in the last twenty years. My rollercoasters have been fast, slow, crazy, but they have been steady. They have been steady enough to allow me to see my surroundings. Many of us are afraid to open our eyes during the rollercoaster ride, but to be accomplished or successful, you must open your eyes, see everything surrounding the rollercoaster, listen to the screams and laughs, feel the wind, and smell the fear all at the same time.

To accomplish your goals, you must know where your happy place is so that you can sit and visualize and take time to write out your plans and what success means and looks like to you!

#ThisThingCalledLife -Task #9- In the upcoming days, take a moment to find your happy place. When you find this place, try to frequent it at least once a week. As you continue to frequent this place, create goals for yourself and place them up in this place.

CHAPTER 10

Just Reflect

I plan to do my best and learn from the mistake I have made, will continue to make, and pay attention to those that are placed in my life to assist me.

There is nothing in stores or on the World Wide Web to direct us on how to deal with #ThisThingCalledLife. Well, there are those self-help books, but there is no particular guide that provides solid guidance on coping with everything we all go through.

No one person can help us cope with the issues either. This is a problem that many do not understand. We are supposed to go through issues. We are supposed to fail, struggle, cry, be heart broken. I don't care what anyone says, but we are supposed to face challenges and it's good for us; it builds character. It also helps us to be the person we are destined to be. It teaches us how to appreciate the good things. The trials teach us ... or rather should teach us how to deal with everyday things. The struggles of life will never go away, but with every struggle there is a good; you just have to sit still, and it will be revealed.

My 2018 was a year of sitting still. My 2018 was not just centered on self-reflection but embracing pain that I've never felt before. It was a year of cleansing my soul. It was a year of being vulnerable, but also learning who to be vulnerable to. This year taught me the true meaning of friendship. I am always receiving compliments about my light shining, which was reason why people gravitated towards me, lying just to get close to me and turning out to be evil. I couldn't understand that before, but 2018 showed me that. From co-workers who had their own agendas and were deceitful, to people who I trusted to share personal things or my space with and were not who they claimed to be. My son always tells me I'm too trusting (I guess he gets that from his grandfather), and I finally understood this.

My journey was for me. My jungle experience is just mine. My journey was not for anyone to know about unless I elected to share. It was not for anyone to judge me and if they did; who freaking cares! It was not for anyone to give me advice because I needed to embrace all of my pain! I needed to embrace it all! I needed to be still and see pay attention to the good that was coming and that is still coming!

We are destined to go through painful events. Late summer, I called my first husband and thanked him. Who does that, right? We had an extremely simple marriage that ended because we were an inexperienced, young couple who didn't know how to fight for each other or really the importance of family structure. We really had no business getting married because we didn't know who we were. But society said we should because we had a baby together. We were simply unsure of who we were. I changed my major five or ten times in college. I was supposed to be a dentist and he was supposed to be.... definitely not the cop that he has been for 14 or 15 years. But we fell in love, had a baby, got married, and realized that we didn't even know who we were, what we wanted to do, or how to get there. For some, it would have been ideal to do this together, but for us we elected to separate and find ourselves. It wasn't that simple though. But we broke up, well went through the divorce process and went to counseling. He even wrote me the sweetest card reminding me that it wasn't my fault or his. We just had to find ourselves. It made me think of that Donnell Jones song I use to sing all of the time in his red car; Where I Wanna Be.

There were many hard days and nights, but we respected each other, went to counseling together, and as I look at it now, we actually talked a lot and still do, which helps very much with co-parenting. I learned lots of lessons here and as I reflect on it, he taught me so much. I must love myself to ever love anyone else. I cannot grow with anyone if I don't even have my own plan.

I needed this, even though I didn't know it then. My first ex-husband respects me. He respected me then. This along with the foundation that my dad had already laid down for me, helped me to see how a woman was/is supposed to be treated. The pain from the divorce was hard. It was definitely not ideal. And ten years ago, when I divorced, I remember going on a work trip with a great friend of mine to Virginia Tech and being able to clearly process what I was going through. I do not remember the conversation or anything outside of us leading a conference that we were supposed to be a part of and me buying white cowboy boots, oh… and her turning me on to that movie…. vampire…. werewolves….

This trip helped me find clarity.

The irony is; ten years later she is one of my best friends and she sent me this text yesterday, "What is pain? The manifestation of the physical expression of any form of physical, emotional, spiritual, and or psychological trauma." Dr. Donela Wright further shared in her text that "pain is uncomfortable. It forces a reconciliation between the thing that is hurting and the thing that did the hurt." That's extremely real. It's deep. It takes self-reflection to even understand this. She continued with saying "being able to identify both is part of the battle. Only solitude and deep reflection can facilitate this." 2018 did that for me. I sat in solitude and anyone who truly understands life, understands this is a necessity!

When I left my second ex-husband, I was placed in solitude. I didn't share with many where I was, why I was there, or anything because this was the time for me to hurt. 2018 taught me that in order to grow, I must be able to conquer that task of overcoming something that we are not taught. Remember there is nothing to teach us how to hurt and how to patch ourselves back up. Well, we are taught about prayer, but many do not understand or might not even believe in it. For me, I believe and still do and will always! My faith walk was just amazing!!! I had to be able to do it alone without the words and advice of people who solicit their advice without knowing the whole story. And my alone is obviously without humans.

I had to wait on HIM to guide me. I had to listen and walk even when I was afraid, but I learned how to do this. I had to truly embrace my character even though I was being pushed and hurt. As much as I wanted to be mean sometimes, I had to walk with grace versus trying to hurt a person that I felt hurt me. I had to do it and learn to be vulnerable. I had to cry in solitude. I had to still love a person who was hurting and was hurting others. I had to let God speak through me because this marriage; the ex was not the same as my first.

The latter was hard for me in 2018 because I'm naturally strong. It was hard, because who wants to deal with the task of being weak and feeling like a failure? But this is something that we fail to add to that #ThisThingCalledLife Guide that is nonexistent. How do we learn to cope with hurt? How to we learn to cope with betrayal? How do we do this? Some do it with alcohol. Some do it with drugs. Some do it knowing that God is there to support them. What is the right way?

I can't say that I can truly answer this, but no self-help book (and I've read many) could tell me how to pull myself out of bed when I'm hurting. No self-book could have helped me in 2018 when I needed to be in solitude. I needed more than ever to trust MY faith walk. No person could have helped me the way I helped myself by embracing every single moment.

While I visited Jerusalem for Christmas 2018, we discussed this. In order to grow we agreed, we must embrace the hurt, but we have to know and trust that everything will be ok. In all aspects of our lives we have to believe this. As I walk into 2020 and as I welcome my present, I have learned that emotions are needed for us to grow and to become the humans...person that we are designed to be. Each emotion is a part of our puzzle piece. Last year my puzzle piece of hurt was placed down and it compliments those other puzzle pieces that were already glued down. I embraced the hurt of another divorce. I embraced the hurt of being alone in a foreign place. I embraced the hurt of liars and distrustful people. And as my mentor shared with me prior to my trip, now it's time to let go of all of that Kiera." Not only did I need to understand that my second divorce happened, it was completely opposite of the first on all aspects, but it's a part of my life and I cannot change it.

My mentor left me with this as I was headed to the airport. "I was thinking about our conversation earlier you have a LOT of things REVEALED to you that proves you are not the problem in a relationship. SO, TURN THE KEY

AND LET YOURSELF OUT OF RELATIONSHIP JAIL ."
He further told me to open my heart and there will be
an amazing man that will come into my life just as so
many other amazing things keep coming. His hashtag
#OnlyYou is a reminder that I need everything that I am
faced with. There is always a good. For me, to walk away
and listen to God in 2018 has allowed me to grow in so
many ways. I have lessons on top of lessons on top of
other lessons (hmmm sounds like a rap verse…drop the
beat… ok corny…) this year to guide me. So, my goals
for this upcoming year is to keep listening, understand
that I can't control everything, but what I can control,
do it! And it also taught me not to change! I'm going to
be me and proud of my dope puzzle pieces!

Be happy! Embrace your emotions and most importantly
in 2019, 2020, and moving forward understand that
#ThisThingCalledLife happens and you just need to
embrace the pain!

As Dr. DW says "2019 doesn't have to be the same as
2018."

#ThisThingCalledLife -Task #10- After completing this
last chapter, take moments daily to just reflect. Each
time you feel as if you are being attacked or being a target

of just negativity, write down the good that is there. Remember with every bad, there is a good. Additionally, create your own quote. What quote would assist you with this?

$\mathcal{A}$CKNOWLEDGMENT

I'm thankful for my life! I'm thankful for the discernment that God has given me. I'm thankful for the circle that He has blessed me with.

I cherish the relationships that I have with people. There are two people who are humble souls. I know that after they read this acknowledgement, they are probably going to respond by saying I don't need any recognition, but I cannot move forward without just sharing how blessed I am to have both Avery Fleming and Jason (no middle name) Thompson in my life. Jason and I spent his 21st birthday at the car lot and it was because of me. Prior to that we were already friends, but every time I think of what selfless looks like, that day comes to mind. Thank you Jason. I still don't like you, but I do love you. I wish you and your babies and T nothing but greatness.

Fleming has been important to me since my sophomore year in college. He would pick me up for PT and I would politely answer the phone telling him that I was still sleep! Ha! And nineteen years later we have not missed a beat. I have enough emails and texts between us to write a book on what learning to believe in yourself looks life. He has pushed me even when I roll my eyes on the other side of the phone. He is always positive and has taught me so much about life. He was one of the first people I shared that I was pregnant with and not once did he make me feel that my life was over. He has kept my son and I couldn't see my life without him in it. I'm spoiled and just like my baby girl Cree (love you!) if he doesn't answer, I'm throwing a tantrum. I call until he answers and for that (yeah yeah...) I love you!

Cree, I cannot wait to see all that will happen with you! Jordan K, you are one who inspires me too! (Was that discreet Jordan??, ha!).

Continue being you and thank you for your support . I think the world of both of you.

Louis ... Mr. Acosta thank you for always being my friend who will sit and watch jeopardy with me, share random facts from Readers Digest, and after my weekend with you receiving VIP in studios just because we are inquisitive. Those many phone calls answering "what" obviously gave us a strong bond!

I'm thankful for those that wrote my forward! The stories that I have about us showcase this: my circle is DOPE! It also showcases what love looks like. I've learned after moving six times in six years that we are special. I love and appreciate you Tikela (I love you and I mean it!). Thank you for sharing Aubrey and Addie and even Twon with me!

You are my favorite son Anthony Shaun! I appreciate you for being so resilient, being my "son"shine on many cloudy days. Thank you for loving me and even sharing me! I can't wait to see what God has in store for you! Always remember who you are and give things your all! It's never enough to just be kind and nice.... Laziness is a disease and the only disease you have is T1D which I'm praying a cure will be found one day soon!

Tinka Boo! Thank you for my daily prayers! I wish you continue to see and know the light that you bring! Mr. Warren Fort, knowing your story and receiving your texts inspire me. You are a fighter and I'm glad to know you. I can't wait to read both you and Ms. Cherry's book!

Charles, since Cinnabon, we have had a great relationship. Even when I have not always been mature enough to deal with issues, you have shown me that you love me and have repaid me with prayers, consistency, and an open door. Thanks for sharing Jen and my boys!

Jayla boo!!! Law school would have been much harder without you calling me and taking to me on the way home. Our relationship is beautiful and while I'm suppose to be the mentor, thank you for being the mentor on days that I just don't want to adult!

Thank you mom and dad!! I have so many great characteristics because of you! I'm sending love to my only blood sister, Kevonda and I pray she sees just how much she has to give this world.

My cousin Pooh! Thank you for the morning prayers and being the glue for our family. We have a great family, but like any family there are things to work on so that we can grow. Can you imagine if everyone conquered their dreams? Well, I can see it happening and you Pooh are that person whose prayers push us to succeed. Keep being amazing!

My circle is dope because we understand the need to grow together and check on each other! I love you Jen! You are exactly right (notice I had to separate you and Charles), but it was meant for me to meet him so I can have you in my life. OMG!! Through my tantrums and my selfish moments, and even those many times I doubt things, you remind me to keep it in that God box and walk away. You teach me how to forgive, how to focus on the good, while just trusting. Thanks for never judging me and my crazy moments....

Attorney Christine Hart, I am so happy I took that Saturday class! You are such a blessing lady bug! I love my messages from you and thank you for believing in me and pushing me through the storm. You did it so subtle that I don't even realize I knew what you were doing! I love you beautiful lady!

Adrienne thanks for pushing me in our younger years and giving me amazing God kids. I watch from afar and I'm thankful. I'm thankful for Daivon too April and I'm proud of the accomplishments of both of you.

Desmond!!!!!!!! I said that in my loud squeaky voice for you! From those loud crazy moments, to the many genuine conversations we have, I want you to keep moving in the direction of your heart. Thanks for allowing me to be a part of the Kemp family! I love y'all!

I was able to blog about great black men and women and I thank you! I watch your social media pages and you all inspire me! KayBEE and Erica!!! Thank you! That buss trip to Berlin (tropical island) was one of the highlights of my time overseas!

Lisa and Quentin...thank you! Lisa.... there is just not enough to say about the many many many conversations we have all of the time.

Mariam and Yulunda...thank you sisters! My journey would not even have this beautiful ending without you two. You both are just amazing women and I cannot wait for a trip with you!

Tosha and Shalanda ...oh the laughs cleansed my soul! Tosha... Jerusalem was one of my top trips and I don't think I've ever laughed that hard! I am mailing you pictures and you better frame them.

My DST line sisters. My Tina! That summer made me reflect and I'm so thankful for you! My TBS line sisters! Contella, thank you! Thank you and Will for opening your doors for me. Shonte boo boo!! Thank you for the same! Thanks Mike and I can't wait to see how Big you become! Thank you both for giving me a new brother; Dave. His words via text always come on time!

Terrell, Sharonda, Donela I appreciate and love you all!

Sharonda, thank you for your beautiful cards and I am so happy for your new journey.

Terrell, I can't wait to see where God takes you. I never got your autograph, but I feel I need to.

Donela, thank you for my nephew! Thank you for sharing Pam (well you have NO choice!)! And thank you both for including me in your family! Both Anthonys are going to be success stories! We will NOT have it another way!

Charlene!! Thank you for being an amazing friend! Thank you for my videos and thank you for uplifting me! I pray I give you what you give me! You are a great mom and I learn so much from you and your tenacity for life!

Todgi!! This cover is so dope!! Trina Logan, my time with you this summer recharged me!

Teha Roche' each time I spend with you is beyond amazing! I cherish our friendship, your words, the fun that we have, and your willingness to never judge and trust me! I love you girlfriend!!

I thank you Mike for being a great dad for Anthony and trusting me to take him on my journey called life! We have done an amazing job co-parenting and I could not have asked for a better father for my child.

I have so many amazing mentors; Treana, Melanie, Mr. Springs, of course Fleming and so many others who teach me!

Dr. Treana, thank you for supporting me like I am your own!

Renee and Merita, thank you! Thank you for learning me and trusting me before you knew me. The eyes really tell your story!

My mentees... especially Mr. Julian who I know is trying to make me his case study. It's not going to happen!

My Regina I love you baby. Please know that you are so strong and you push me to be better! Your random messages make my day! Ginaya, you are actually my big sister and I love you girlFRAND!!

Sopphire, keep being great! I have so many and they all know I love them! K.G. Ruff, thank you for our words. I remember a car talk we had many years ago and it still resonates with me.

Faye and James, that night I stayed with you both and those prayers...OMG!

Keni Hines, thank you for teaching me how to enjoy life and allowing me to be me. From 18 to now, we have always been able to pick up and laugh and laugh some more!

I thank everyone who is in my life and please charge my mind and not my heart if you are not on this page! You are important!

I'm blessed to have so many and I am so thankful to Our Father for always supporting me as I felt like the book of Job, Jonah, and Habakkuk. I trust my rollercoaster rides and I trust you. I am thankful for each encounter even though they suck....but I embrace them.

Made in the USA
Monee, IL
07 November 2019